SCIENCE STARTERS
Matter

by Carolyn Bernhardt

BELLWETHER MEDIA • MINNEAPOLIS, MN

Note to Librarians, Teachers, and Parents:

Blastoff! Readers are carefully developed by literacy experts and combine standards-based content with developmentally appropriate text.

Level 1 provides the most support through repetition of high-frequency words, light text, predictable sentence patterns, and strong visual support.

Level 2 offers early readers a bit more challenge through varied simple sentences, increased text load, and less repetition of high-frequency words.

Level 3 advances early-fluent readers toward fluency through increased text and concept load, less reliance on visuals, longer sentences, and more literary language.

Level 4 builds reading stamina by providing more text per page, increased use of punctuation, greater variation in sentence patterns, and increasingly challenging vocabulary.

Level 5 encourages children to move from "learning to read" to "reading to learn" by providing even more text, varied writing styles, and less familiar topics.

Whichever book is right for your reader, Blastoff! Readers are the perfect books to build confidence and encourage a love of reading that will last a lifetime!

This edition first published in 2019 by Bellwether Media, Inc.

No part of this publication may be reproduced in whole or in part without written permission of the publisher. For information regarding permission, write to Bellwether Media, Inc., Attention: Permissions Department, 6012 Blue Circle Drive, Minnetonka, MN 55343.

Library of Congress Cataloging-in-Publication Data

Names: Pettiford, Rebecca, author.
Title: Matter / by Rebecca Pettiford.
Description: Minneapolis, MN : Bellwether Media, Inc., 2019. | Series: Blastoff! Readers. Science Starters
  | Includes bibliographical references and index. | Audience: 5-8. | Audience: K to 3.
Identifiers: LCCN 2017061626 (print) | LCCN 2018009246 (ebook) | ISBN 9781681035437 (ebook)
  | ISBN 9781626178106 (hardcover ; alk. paper) | ISBN 9781618914668 (pbk. ; alk. paper)
Subjects: LCSH: Matter–Juvenile literature. | Matter–Properties–Juvenile literature.
Classification: LCC QC173.36 (ebook) | LCC QC173.36 .P483 2019 (print) | DDC 530.4–dc23
LC record available at https://lccn.loc.gov/2017061626

Editor: Christina Leaf   Designer: Josh Brink

Printed in the United States of America, North Mankato, MN

Table of Contents

Matter on a Cold Day

You put on your coat and step outside. It is so cold you can see your breath. Snow melts into water droplets on your gloves.

4

Do you know what your coat, your breath, and water droplets have in common? They are all matter!

What Is Matter?

Everything is matter! Matter is made up of tiny parts called **atoms**. Atoms join together to make **molecules**.

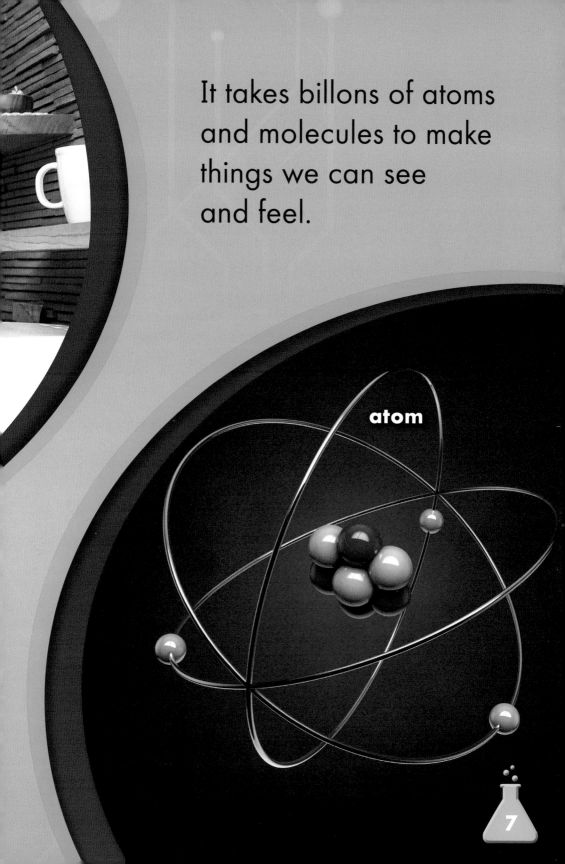

It takes billons of atoms
and molecules to make
things we can see
and feel.

atom

All matter has **mass**.
Mass is the amount of
matter in something.

Matter also has **volume**. Volume is the space that matter occupies.

States of Matter

liquid

solid

Matter can exist in three possible states. It can be a **solid**, a **liquid**, or a **gas**.

For example, liquid water and solid ice are the same type of matter. It can also be a gas called vapor.

vapor

Solids hold their shape. Their molecules are tightly packed.

If you put shells in a jar,
they do not mold to the
jar's shape. The shells
cannot change size,
and their volume is fixed.

Liquid molecules are less tightly packed. They can take the shape of a container.

If you pour syrup on pancakes, it spreads out. But it still has the same volume.

Most gases are invisible. They fit into big and small spaces. Their molecules move closer together or farther apart to fit the space.

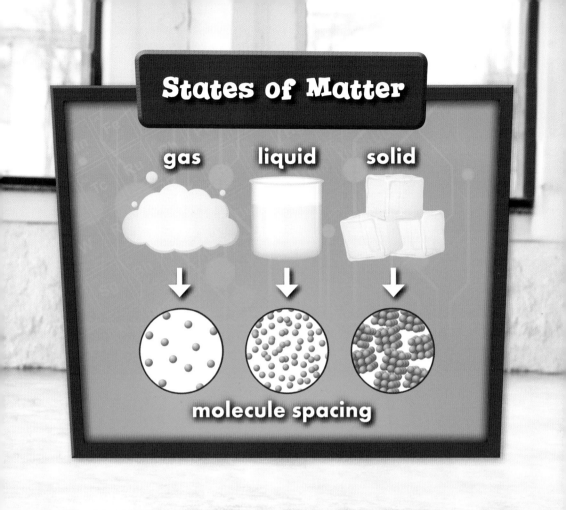

States of Matter

gas   liquid   solid

molecule spacing

For example, if you press on a ball, the space gets smaller. However, the amount of air has not changed.

Matter can change its state when **energy**, such as heat, is added or taken away. Adding heat can turn a solid into a liquid and a liquid into a gas. You can turn a liquid into a solid by cooling it.

Solid, Liquid, and Gas

You can see matter changing states at home!

What you will need:

- a glass bowl
- a cup of ice cubes
- a pot

---

1. Fill a bowl with the ice.

2. Think about ways you can change the solid ice to liquid water. Heat energy is the fastest way. You can let the ice melt at room temperature. You can place the bowl in the sun.

3. Once you have liquid, pour it into a pot.

4. Ask an adult to help you boil it on the stove. Now it will become a gas!

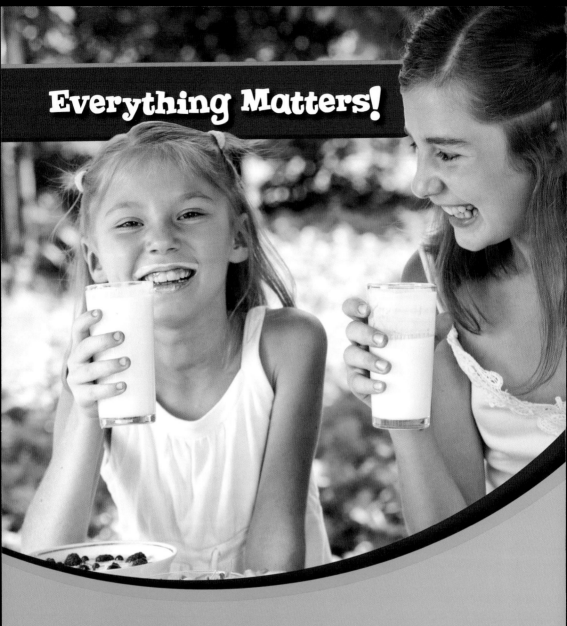

We need solids, liquids, and gases to live. We eat solids. We drink liquids. We breathe gas.

Understanding matter helps us understand the world around us!

Glossary

atoms—units of one of the basic substances that make up the planet; atoms make up everything in the universe.

energy—useable power that allows things to be active

gas—matter that does not keep its size or shape

liquid—matter that flows freely but stays the same size

mass—how much material an object has

molecules—the smallest parts of substances that still act like the substance; molecules are made up of two or more atoms joined together.

solid—matter that keeps its size and shape

volume—the space that matter occupies

To Learn More

AT THE LIBRARY
Maurer, Daniel D. *Do You Really Want to Skate on Thin Ice?: A Book About States of Matter.* Mankato, Minn.: Amicus, 2017.

Rompella, Natalie. *Experiments in Material and Matter with Toys and Everyday Stuff.* North Mankato, Minn.: Capstone Press, 2016.

Slade, Suzanne. *Splat!: Wile E. Coyote Experiments With States of Matter.* North Mankato, Minn.: Capstone Press, 2014.

ON THE WEB
Learning more about matter is as easy as 1, 2, 3.

1. Go to www.factsurfer.com.

2. Enter "matter" into the search box.

3. Click the "Surf" button and you will see a list of related web sites.

With factsurfer.com, finding more information is just a click away.

Index

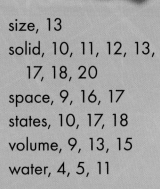

The images in this book are reproduced through the courtesy of: charobnica, front cover (periodic table); John Dakapu, front cover (circuit); pjmorley, front cover (hero); Julza, pp. 4-5; maroke, p. 6; Ruslan Grechka, p. 7; Kletr, p. 8; Gary C. Tognoni, p. 9; MikeLaptev, p. 10; Lesterman, p. 11; RichLegg, p. 12; Evgeniya Lystsova, p. 13; PeopleImages, p. 14; AdamEhPhotographer, p. 15; LightFieldStudios, pp. 16-17; MicroOne, p. 17 (states of matter); Boonrod, p. 18; Tom Begasse, p. 19; Oksana Klymenko, p. 20; Africa Studio, p. 21; PISUTON'c, p. 24.